Quotist

450 Quotes
by Brad

Brad Kong

Disclaimer

The graphics on this book cover is from Edit.org. I use the site to design my covers; it provides book cover templates with its copy-righted images to writers who paid "annual memberships."

I do have three proofs of my **membership** to Edit.org, **payment receipt** for the membership through Paypal and **reference** address to the image of the site. I am writing this because I received emails regarding my "book cover images" twice; both cases were resolved within a day. I decided to stick only to my own or edit.org's images since I cannot keep getting copyright emails. If you have any issue regarding my cover art, feel free to contact me: I will be more than happy to provide the three proofs again.

Also by Brad Kong

Brad Short Story Collection I:

Brad Short Story Collection II:

Brad Short Story Collection III:

Brad Short Story Collection I & II
Why Are Orcas Friendly to Humans?
30 Reasons Why I am Lucky
30 Little Things Making Me Happy

Quotist:

Quotist I
Quotist II
Quotist III
Quotist IV
Quotist V
Quotist

Prologue

"Quotist" means a *quote artist*. These are *quotes* about my random thoughts, analyses, practical knowledge, *useful info* you probably didn't know, or *interesting facts* I have run into, occasionally.

I hope you will enjoy them and they will give you more insights into your life.

Quotist

450 Quotes
by **Brad**

1. Fart represents *power hierarchy* in a group. Whenever there are more than three people, whoever *fart* comfortably is the *supreme* one.

2. When we act modestly when we don't have to, our decency comes out.

3. Most people assume that "Rocky (1976)" is the first film Sylvester Stallone starred in – wrong! In Wikipedia, I actually counted that it's the *18th* movie he has appeared or taken a role in. Not giving up is the key to success.

4. Along with our fundamental eating and sleeping desires, humans have an unrecognized desire to trust or believe in something unconditionally. Religions have taken advantage of it, too.

5. Frequently, **owning** and spending **money**, rather than being short of it, **causes a problem**.

6. The other day, I watched a relationship expert say, "Women never want to be a man's only goal." Instinctively, I believe *a woman doesn't choose a man* if *she feels that she is too good* for him.

7. In that sense, "love between men and women" is merely a non-existing fantasy. There are more calculations and transactions than emotions *in mating*.

8. Instead of chasing women, just *do your job.* There is no visible advantage to being in a relationship than being single, unless you prefer confinement to freedom.

9. The girl (or boy) you are obsessed with is not a special one – *Never!* According to a dating expert, idealization is a basic *psychological step* in the *forming stage* of a relationship. In other words, people just idealize their partners based on no reason when they are in love.

10. Getting too much money all at once can be a **curse**. We need to be the most careful, right after something "too good to be true" happens.

11. Subconsciously, no one is happy after spending money. Spending is a kind of loss, technically; many of what we buy is pointless these days. Everyone feels depraved, after losing "resources to survive," after all.

12. **Saving** money and living frugally is **not for finance** – it's for mental peace. When we show lavish spendings, we can be physically attacked, too.

13. There is *no point* living extremely *diligently and proficiently.* We won't get *a medal of honor* from heaven *after we die.*

14. Some work blindly hard and save since they believe money has an "absolute value" – it does not! It's merely a social promise, which has been *broken regularly* throughout history.

15. We don't have to be good at everything. In fact, we don't have to be the best at anything.

16. "Keeping a few little joys" can **save** our **lives**. Little joys don't have to be expensive – for example, it can be something like browsing the internet, reading a comic or eating a tasty slice at your favorite pizzeria. When harsh moments come, those <u>little fun</u> will sustain your life.

17. Writing is not exactly delightful fun to me, but it brings me *meaning*. In other words, I feel I waste the whole day (again) whenever I don't write anything. I feel *fulfilled* when I write something or publish a book.

18. Some experts encourage people to have more failures and suggest "failing a lot" means getting close to success. In real life, <u>repeated failure</u> or hardships (or even one) can <u>discourage</u> a person<u> for life</u>. For example, I failed my "small business" *only once* and don't plan to open another store for life.

19. I believe "accumulating small successes" can be a better life strategy. Get a driver's license. Finish an online course and win an easy certificate. Complete doable quests. Aim achievable targets.

20. Chances don't come all the time – whatever it is, it could be "the only or last" opportunity.

21. **The environment is stronger than will.** I read that Brazil had six times bigger slave trades than the USA by the 19th century; I thought that maybe Brazilians are bad or the country demanded

it for bigger agriculture. Nonetheless, did you know that Brazil is much nearer to Africa than North America is? The truth is **the easternmost point of Brazil is closer to Africa than to its westernmost point.** If you need to read more books, move to an area close to a library. If you want to quit alcohol, move into a place restricting booze. Environment is "the most powerful factor" and always wins.

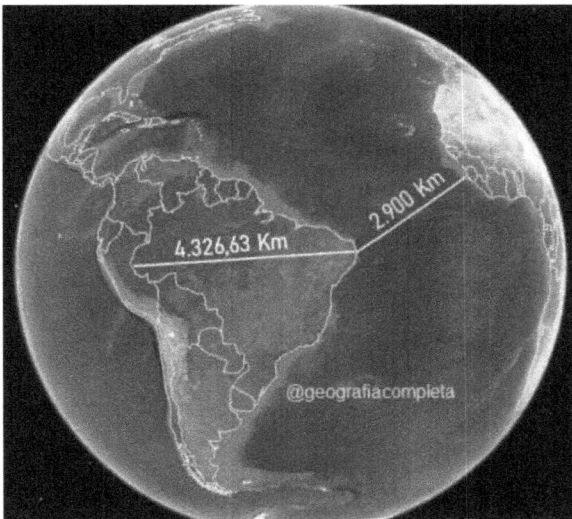

22. Often, the most expensive *medical bills* for a lot of people are dental *receipts* (even for healthy people). Taking care of teeth can save you literally a ton of money throughout life.

23. Taking care of teeth always starts with "not eating" *sugary* foods. Remember this rule for your dental health: Not taking harmful food (70%); daily care, including brushing and flossing

(20%); dentist (10%). Dentists are necessary and helpful, but they **won't** be able to <u>bring</u> your natural <u>teeth back</u>.

24. Among all dishes in the world, it seems <u>Thai foods</u> are the most <u>detrimental</u> to teeth. As far as I know, it's almost the only country *putting sugar* directly into their *main dishes*. The *healthiest* are <u>salads</u> (preferably, without a dressing), according to my experience.

25. One of the most excellent ways to get out of smartphone addiction without hurting functionality is <u>buying a cheaper android phone</u>, instead of expensive iPhones. I used to own a free LG phone for 6 years. Lately, I got a new Blu 4 for $30 and don't like it as much. I notice that I check my phone *far less* than before, even though the functionality of it is advanced.

26. No one cares about you as much as you assume. *They are all busy with their lives.* So *stop worrying* about what others think about you.

27. **Happiness** is merely *a <u>tool</u> to extend a life* – <u>not the purpose</u> of a life. Being consistently happy is not possible.

28. Women are generally more deceptive than men, according to my experience – never trust the tears of women. The best way to find a future bride is checking her capabilities and achievements so far (check which school she graduated from or how much she makes a year). Do not check her past relationships, virginity or chastity, as a lot of stupid Korean men do – these can be all lies. I notice that Korean boys are usually concerned with those, which is *pointless*.

29. American writers commonly show their photos in their books, while Koreans hardly do. When I think about it, writing is one of the professions where we don't necessarily have to show our faces, especially online. Unless there is a *clear advantage,* keeping our privacy protected is wise.

30. It's *unfair* that advertising is getting more impactful than products we make these days. When you think about it, social media postings are all about advertisements.

31. I have thought that working means making money. Weirdly, being able to gather people means *making dough* nowadays. I personally believe it's not fair that boisterous talkers make more than honest laborers.

32. **Sugar** is *the worst enemy* in our real lives. It's something we need to fight against until we die.

33. I personally believe *humans* can be evils or angels, solely depending on the environmental situation. For example, Jewish are Holocaust victims and slaughterers to Palestinians at the same time. Ukrainians are Jewish killers during World War II and victims from the late Russian invasion. Russians tried to save a cat evicted from a Siberian train the other day in 2024, but also shot rockets into Ukrainian terrain in the same year. There is no good or bad side, after all: *This is how humans are.*

34. I watched a YouTube video about *Feng Shui* the other day. The old master said, "We *shouldn't* live in a house *bigger* than we need. Otherwise, wealth leaks out through the door."

35. The Korean Feng Shui master strongly suggested <u>moving out</u> of your place <u>if bad things keep happening</u> for more than three years. Personally, I had a hard time while I was staying in Buffalo, NY for my college. All the painful things happened to me in NY State (including NYC), in general.

36. In Illinois, I shouldn't have stayed in my business location for eight years – it was a dead retail location. I still liked the cheaper rent there and we made most of our profits from online sales, though (specifically, on eBay, then). In the end, the plaza owner brought a loud business named Jazzercise next door. I got a rent discount for the noise reason, but had to close out my business as soon as the lease contract was over. Conclusively, I made way more money after closing out the business in 2014.

37. Life is all about making choices, continuously. Nonetheless, a lot of businesses seem to believe that change is a good thing no matter what – wrong! I think it's important to *keep the good choices,* and throw out or adjust the bad ones. In my case, I think I may stay in my current condo for long, since it has been a fine choice. I *may* change only my career if it doesn't work out forever.

38. There is *no cure* for stupid people. Don't try to solve their impossible problems. You don't have any obligation to solve theirs, to begin with.

39. If you are an author, the best way to make your book vivid is taking *real examples.* It is easier for readers to understand and more interesting for authors to write.

40. You *can't hurry* reading, writing or publishing. We have to entangle our words out slowly.

41. In the stock market, there is one sure way to avoid fraud. Try to buy stocks from a company whose product you are using (for example, you are using an Amazon product named Kindle now).

42. Israelis are bombing themselves now by attacking Palestinians since 2023. *Hurting others must come back to the offenders.* Besides, they cannot beat the "United States of Arab Bothers" alone. People may feel less sorry for them if the next holocaust arrives.

43. There is no perfect book – but there are always better writings.

44. Internet *trolls* are *losers*. Some don't even know how to post their Amazon ratings anonymously, instead of writing reviews with their names.

45. If we stay impoverished for too long, indigence will stick to our lives hard like superglue – poverty can be our *destinies* that way.

46. I believe *paying more tax* is better than *donating money somewhere else* and getting tax-exempt. First of all, I don't have to worry about IRS tax audits. Second, it makes my finances *simpler* overall.

47. Being fat is actually a good thing. It means human bodies are so efficient that we can live for long on a little amount of food.

48. In real life, there are the major two lethal weapons we carry – one is **calmness** and the other is **persistence**.

49. If you want to look pretty, just lose weight, above all. Sometimes, people don't have to do anything else, including getting plastic surgeries or even buying new make-ups.

50. *Smart* people never get caught by the police: Why? Above all, many *don't commit crime*, to begin with – they obviously know it's hard to escape from anything these days.

51. People in prison are not just bad – frankly, they are stupid, too.

52. **I believe *hoarders* are *lonely people*.** Feeling lonely is similar to feeling empty, void or missing. So they tend to fill up their spaces with more stuff.

53. It's common sense that alcohol causes severe depression, resulting in suicides, occasionally. I believe the alcohol industry is huge and powerful enough to mask the fact.

54. *Lonely death* is the death of a person living alone, which is *increasing* in Korea. Police always find *soju* (common diluted vodka) without exception in the victims' residences in the country.

55. It seems humans create reasons *to be angry* or fight all the time. Probably, that has benefited our survival, to some extent, which is not absolutely necessary any more. When you are angry

next time, just remember *it's mere instinct*, which has nothing to do with logic or situations.

56. There are two types of crimes: **crimes with** and **without profit.** Robbery is a crime with profit (for offenders). Taking drugs is a crime without profit. *Losers* tend to commit *crimes without profit* more.

57. Alicia Kincheloe (30) worked at her father's mechanics and found a raccoon in their dumpster one day in 2022. She poured gasoline, burned the raccoon alive, took a Tik Tok video and posted it online. She was found guilty of animal cruelty and was *officially sentenced* to a $2,500 fine and 100 hours of community service. This type of crime doesn't benefit anyone. Shoplifts at least benefit the offender financially, but she only lost cash and got a criminal record. By the way, to me, the worst sentence she got in this case is showing her name, face, location and her father's business all over online, which won't disappear forever.

58. "Going to the gym" is such a waste. Most people don't walk to the grocery store and carry some food; they squander gas all along and throw away their physical energy, membership fee and electricity at the gym, instead.

59. Carlos was a *horrible* boss in my previous nursing home job. He was a short Mexican sous chef and tried to make everything good for the organization, while converting all the employees into enemies. In common sense, sous chef is a no big deal position with *meager wage,* but I assume he thought he is higher ranked above cooks and dishwashers. He was not exactly a criminal, but

stupidly hurt others without gaining any benefit to anyone. Thanks to him, I finally decided to become a writer.

60. Some women, especially those wealthy whites from Hampton, seem to *mistakenly think* their husband won't cheat if they get vaginal plastic surgeries after giving birth – *a huge misunderstanding* to me (as I am a man). If home meals are good, you never eat out? Cheaters will be cheaters for any reason.

61. Not eating is always right. When you have a choice, always go for it. Eating three times a day is crazily a lot and often. *The best way to lose weight is eating only dinners* – one meal a day. To me, this has been the practical way to eat less – I have lost 45 pounds without making a specific effort since 2020.

62. While I was eating at Taco Bell the other day, I noticed that an old Indian couple couldn't figure out how to order via its electronic kiosk, so they had to order with the cashier. *When we don't use our brains, these get worse.* Eventually, we can get into dementia that way in the end.

63. Often, there is no practical need to make *more money* than now – it is just our greed that wants more.

64. I write more or even better when I don't think about publishing. I can *write freely* when I don't worry about success – similarly, I just cannot write if I try to write a masterpiece selling well. Greed, popularity concerns or ambitions are all obstacles to creation.

65. The *enemy* of trying is *perfection*.

66. Is global warming really a bad thing? I have no interest in having winter for a little longer every year. Be suspicious of everything!

67. I see more *pigeons* are living *under the filthy bridges* in the city *than pleasant gardens* in the suburbs. As far as I can see, *they have options* to fly away, but they haven't. We have to see if we live that way, although we have an option to get out to better places.

68. "As much as we cannot avoid misfortunes, we cannot avoid luck, either." – Anonymous

69. We don't have to take revenge on trolls. They will lose, suffer and go extinct *on their own*. The biggest reason why I despise internet trolls is I have to witness waste.

70. In modern days, 90% of what we are doing has nothing to do with survival. Less than 20% of people actually think and move by his or her own ideas.

71. There are plenty of reasons to divorce. Here is the only way to stay in a marriage. *When we determine not to divorce, we won't divorce.*

72. Money doesn't guarantee happiness. However, lack of money may guarantee misery.

73. Why did McDonald brothers make only $2 millions by selling their business in the 1960s, even though they could have made

$100 millions every year as a royalty? The desire for *instant cash* made them blind.

74. How many children do you need to have? **"Fewer" than you can afford.** This is *the only right answer*.

75. Making money *always* comes with *pain* – every job or business has brought it, according to my experience.

76. We need to be *poor* to be productive. Alternatively, we can live as if we don't own much money. That will make our lives prolific.

77. Have you ever wondered why you are struggling? It may not be a coincidence or destiny. There are mandatory reasons, especially when we live in a wealthy country.

78. Ignorance (under-education) and poverty must hurt others. Being stupid is as bad as being evil in reality.

79. **It is a problem, only when you think it is a problem.** If you consider it's not an issue, it is not.

80. A lot of individual stock traders have never read a single finance book. Often, I can see that obviously without asking a question.

81. Most investors, especially those Korean wives in America, don't read any finance books at all and fail to trade big in the market (I have witnessed them losing unbelievable amounts).

82. William Faukner once said, "The past is never dead. It's not even past." I translated it as saying that life is too short, so we cannot divide it into past, present and future.

83. In 2024, Trump was ordered to pay $83.3 million USD to Jean Carroll by court for rape charge, which happened three decades ago. *The past* is never just the past; it *can cost a lot* of money now.

84. Everyone is trying. In a sense, eating a lot is also trying hard, too. I guess people do their best their own way.

85. There was one time the show host Ellen ordered pizzas during the Oscar award ceremony in 2014. I saw all those Hollywood stars eating pizza deliciously. It was *the first moment* I wondered, "What's the point of making a lot of money?" Rich and poor people eat pizzas altogether in America, anyway.

86. Sleep is the most crucial for our health. Most people do not realize it, only because we do it everyday.

87. Also, sleeping is the best way to *let hard times pass* "without spending extra money" – which is the reason why I let or even encourage my wife to sleep enough, rather than doing anything else. Physiologists insist that it increases our life spans, too. A TED instructor said sleep provides humans superpower. I guess going to bed early guarantees the maximum hours of sleep.

88. I didn't know Franz Kafka had two jobs and wrote novels late at night after work. Apparently, he suffered from lack of sleep throughout his life. He died of tuberculosis at 40. I suspect his

lack of sleep made his immune system weak and caused early death, eventually. Instead of going to a nursing home to spend extra, he should have slept more at home.

89. A successful Japanese cartoonist confessed that he has slept at least 10 hours a day for life and that is the source of his creativity and longevity. He was in his 80s at the time of the interview and said his colleagues who worked overnight mostly died in their 60s.

90. No one can predict anything in the stock market! At least, my forecasts have been wrong all along. Which is the reason why I have invested in dividends and interests, which has been consistent and reasonably successful.

91. When you buy a house, check if it has a library nearby. That's the most important thing to make sure, but most do not check it.

92. The most corrupt organization in America may be HOA (Homeowner's association). First of all, to me, it's very unclear where they spend money exactly (2.5 M budget a year in case of our complex). I see that our *condo office lady* is not available all the time and doesn't work hard (I see she tries to work as little as possible). While I am not happy with them, *I just don't see any way to change them.*

93. While I am not happy with my condo completely, I just don't see an alternative housing option to move to. Most people do not know this, but the property tax of a residential house in America is over 10 times more expensive than that in South Korea. Anywhere I go would have HOA, as it increases its territory to single family

homes these days. I just don't feel like spending more on housing than now.

94. Even if you don't have a Costco membership card, you can enter its food court section after letting its employee know. We can use any credit card to buy a pizza ($2 in 2024) or other menus there. It would be cheaper than dining in other restaurants.

95. When you think about it, *70% of our spending is not necessary*. For example, we can live without a TV, which will only fry your eyes longer.

96. Literally, no one can be dead by hunger any more. Nevertheless, a lot of people (especially men) die or go deep in *trouble* because of *sexual desires*.

97. Troy LaFerrara (42) was a newly-wed civil engineer in Lycoming County, Pennsylvania in 2013; he had finished college and acquired a couple licenses for his profession. One day, he responded to a Craiglists' dating ad – he planned to meet the 19-year-old girl named Miranda Barbour and pay her $100 for her lewd service. Then, she lured him into her SUV in the mall parking lot. In the SUV, her boyfriend was hidden under a blanket on the backseat in advance and both attacked LaFerrara to death; his body was found in a residential backyard the next day; the couple eventually was caught and got life sentences in prison in 2015. Sexual desire is the man's worst enemy – sometimes, we are the ones killing ourselves.

98. There is nothing like perfect timing. You will never be completely ready. Just do it now.

99. In real life, **waiting a little longer** solves a lot of problems.

100. I closed out my video game store almost 10 years ago in 2014. Still I get nightmares related to it now in 2024 (usually, it's about someone stealing games or complaining about not having a title). Making money always has come with pain. *If you have enough,* the first thing you need to do is free yourself from work.

101. I believe the *root* of wealth is from the Sun. Thanks to *sunlight*, we have been able to grow crops. I believe the most ancient and fundamental wealth is from the *accumulation of harvests.*

102. Basically, money is from other people. Then it may not be a perfect strategy to try to get a lot of money from one person (e.g., salary from a boss). Rather, it may be better to get a tiny amount of money from myriads of people, as the human population is over 8 billion now in 2024 (virtually, unlimited). This is why typically *businessmen make more* than employees.

103. Korea has its own unique alphabet called "Hangul." Not only that, more weirdly, the country has its *own* independent words for nearly everything. For example, Koreans call social media "SNS (social networking services)." Also there is a new word called "short form," meaning short contents like Tik tok videos or YouTube shorts. Also, Korean paperback books come with *extra bottom covers* lately to protect, which I haven't seen anywhere else in the world.

104. Virtually, all the Korean men don't have a mustache in the country. They think it's not sanitary, which is often true, to be honest.

105. Most men envy a guy having a lot of girlfriends. But it's *funny* that there is absolutely *no man* who *envies a guy having* a large family or *a lot of children* to support. Scoring a woman can be a bad thing in that sense. To me, the surest way to *live miserably* is *having multiple children,* which may come with a

little bit of joy and fulfillment. But it also brings *a lot of* pain, patience and physical chores. Worst of all, we cannot reverse it when situations go bad later on and no one will pay the parents for the extra work.

106. There are things we must do (e.g., making money). Also, there are things we'd better not do forever (e.g., option trading, gambling, drinking, etc) or do it as late as possible (e.g., having a child). There was a Salvadorian girl server named Vanessa and, apparently, she does only the second and third things without doing the first (making money or going to college), according to her Facebook. Hopeless people repeat their *poor* parents' lives one more time without making any progress – despite having opportunities their parents didn't.

107. Forced to give out the second child (or any number of children after one) can be the source of all the sufferings. *A lot of people blindly think having two children is ideal and do it as if that's mandatory.* Maybe it's just me, but I have seen so many families whose 2nd child causes troubles, while their first one is fine.

108. The best way to *avoid fraud* is *living frugally*. When we live modestly, we may suffer less from money shortage, and less likely we will have a need to get into a crazy scam. Most con-artists use victims' financial desperation and greed.

109. Image is everything: I have listened to several operas lately and feel like a lot of French composers are *undervalued* (e.g., Bizet, Saint-Saëns, etc). It's the same as German painters being

undervalued. As a result, the prejudice has been like Germany (music) vs France (art) – a simple *misconception.*

110. I believe prejudices were created to process our daily lives fast. We can make less profits because of them, too.

111. *Most stress* originates from *financial worries* these days; most financial worries are from having a debt. Conclusively, not having a debt is priceless.

112. While we don't notice, our society is made easier for a family of four people (or less). In restaurants, most tables have four chairs. Most cars have maximum seats of five adults. Most hotels don't allow more than four people to stay in a room. When I think about it, my family lives on Uber without owning a car, because it has three people. A family of five cannot live on Uber since most cars don't have six seats. From having more than three *children,* social inconveniences start.

113. Most men do not know this, but a lot of women (maybe most of them) are obsessed with their *fingernails* and check men's nail conditions carefully as well, while dating. I believe the reason is that they do it *instinctively* since nails show men's financial and social status directly. Traditionally, poor people used to do hard physical work and nails have gotten dirty easily.

114. For the same reason, women check the widths of men's shoulders *by instinct* and feel attraction from them. The more we do physical labor, humans' shoulders get wider, which means more food, wealth and protection to women. To women, dating means life and death matter in a sense.

115. Experts estimate that 108 billion humans have been born in the last six million years. About 8 billion are living on Earth now.

116. *Alcoholism* is my personal evolutionary *riddle*. I myself don't drink at all, but alcoholics are supposed to get extinct faster than others due to accidents by now. However, we see them everywhere – way *more than non-alcohol drinkers*. I assume they have been able to produce more offspring somehow.

117. Believe it or not, a lot of women didn't choose their partners and mates carefully as we presume. Many of us were born solely thanks to alcohol, which explains why the current society is drunken and chaotic.

118. People feel happier when they live simpler lives. If we keep simplifying our lives more and more, we will see that the only thing left in the end is just *"breadwinning"* – not traveling, drinking, watching movies, dating, shopping or gambling – but "mere earning and spending on a few essential things," after all. As a Buddhist monk said, maybe it's ok if we worry only about breadwinning *until we die*: Why? Only complications happen when we want more and are moved by other temptations. They bring more spending as well, which must lead us to more worries.

119. Financial excellency (getting rich) is only achievable when we are not easily motivated by temptations. In fact, people get poorer when they are moved easily. In Korea, we call it "having shallow ears."

120. The *end of over-spending* is *suicide*.

121. While I owned the video game store, I had a chance to observe a good number of kid customers. Children making trouble early in the store became troublesome adults later. Some disappeared for years since they were in jail. In human characteristics, 50% from our genetics will never change.

122. The most stupid person I have seen was Chris from the Jazzercise next door in the strip mall in 2012. There used to be an *Internet cafe* next to my video game shop. They were closed out in 2012 and a new fitness business called Jazzercise moved in. In short, the business tortured me with their loud noise, while they didn't make any profit at all themselves (the business actually lost a lot every month). The owner lady was 50 in 2012 and I still believe she was too old to make that kind of mistake.

123. In the strip mall, there was a nice restaurant owner named Waldo. While everyone liked him, I always felt sorry for him since he and his wife Kathy always worked too much for a small amount of profits. I learned that he got married three times and has five children out of the three relationships in total (two, one, and two children from each marriage). I met his eldest daughter one day and felt she is decent. Then, I wondered if his life could have been *less challenging* if he had only one child, to begin with. Who knows if he didn't have to get divorced from his first marriage? I have only one wife and a daughter and prefer to keep it that way.

124. Unfortunately, poor and weak people are not necessarily good ones all the time. In a sense, some are in their hard situation since they have never been decent ones and no one helped them. Be careful when you show your generosity and kindness.

125. "Don't let the internet rush you. *Nobody is posting their failures.*" – *businessmindset101* on Instagram

126. Whether we are online or not, we shouldn't trust everyone all the time – sadly, that everyone includes our parents, too.

127. Regrettably, I have never had a good relationship with my father; both of my parents, who are divorced, are living in Korea, while I live on my own in America now. I am 50 this year, but I see that they are still using their brain to bring me back to Korea for their convenience and advantage. I guess I am not the first human running into this type of problem. *Don't trust your parents* completely – as a parent, I know some use their own children to make more money, regardless of their happiness. *Trust your instinct,* instead!

128. It is *OK* if you disconnect your relationships with your parents permanently. At least, this is perfectly fine, according to the principle of Korean Buddhism. If you are over 20 years old, you have the right to live your life *freely* on your own – as long as you don't bother or hurt others.

129. My father has a fur business in Korea; this dishonest old man keeps implying that I need to move back to Korea to inherit his business. Did you wear a fur coat this winter? Do you even own one? At least, my wife and daughter don't have it or plan to buy one. The truth is *no one wears a fur coat anymore*, especially along with global warming. Regardless, I don't have any intention to do anything with him. Even if it brings me fortune, I don't want to work with him. I have never had a good relationship with him

for my whole life. Moreover, I don't want to make every situation go along with his intention since I have never liked him – *I don't necessarily want him to be happy* since he made me unpleasant so many times. I know this bother will be over only after he dies. I will never do this kind of thing (insisting) to my daughter. I know it will only ruin our relationship.

130. "The best father in the world is the deceased father." – Shintaro Isihara, the educator and former governor of Tokyo

131. When I was a child, I thought that there is a reason for everything adults do: *No, there isn't*. As a middle-aged man, there are a lot of things I will never understand for those *aging retards*. For example, I don't understand why some (Korean) girls had boyish or "out of fashion" old names because of their stupid parents who made them – it took only a minute to choose a nice name for my daughter in my case. (Let's say some girls' names are Billy, Jill or Mary in America in 2024. Why not Taylor?) I watched some French men rent their separate space for college girls in Paris and ask sex for free rent: **Are they crazy?** They can easily get $3,000 a month by renting anything in the city. They can go to massage parlors or whatever every week for probably $100 a week ($400 a month, which makes them still keep $2,600 extra). I have to pay property tax and put up with all the noises, damages and inconvenience via renting. *I will never do it for free* like them. The fulfillment by saving is bigger than other temporary pleasures.

132. There is a Chinese maxim, " 과유불급(過猶不及) :" A little too much is the same as a little less – *I disagree*. According to my

experience, a little less is always *better* than a little more. No one had a problem after eating a little smaller, while plenty had a stomach ache after eating too much. For that reason, I have never envied a person like Angelina Jolie having six kids, as one is more than enough for me. If two children in a family is average, see if you can go for less than that – I guarantee you won't regret it. If you are not sure whether you have to choose a little more or less, *always choose* a little less for anything.

133. If you are a self-publishing writer without a specific deadline, how can you finish your books without delay? In my case, making book covers in advance helped. Once I have a front cover of an ebook, I tend to complete the contents one way or another. This is true for a lot of things. Once a university builds a new building, they end up making new departments to occupy it one way or another. Once we have a bookshelf, we tend to buy books to fill that up.

134. I wonder if farting is a gift from God to make us laugh, occasionally.

135. Sometimes, "not trying anything" is *the biggest loss.* We have limited time left in our lives.

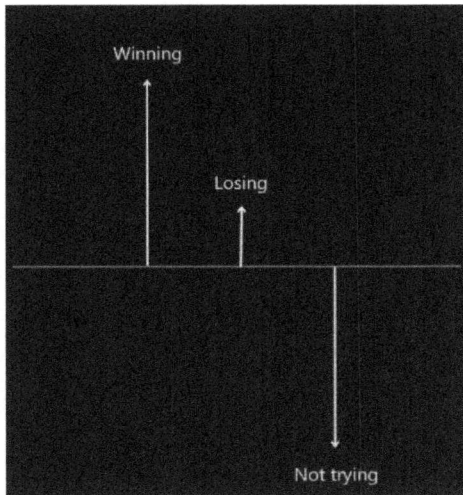

Winning

Losing

Not trying

(image source: visualhustles on Instagram)

136. Nonetheless, according to my experience, not doing anything is better for not damaging current savings, too. I believe building wealth starts from protecting what we have. Do not push yourself to try something all the time – it's OK if you don't do anything as long as you have enough savings – you will lose less this way, overall.

137. "A significant portion of our efficient energy is generated by boiling water these days. Our technological advancements haven't strayed far from the steam age" – HOLUPREDICTIONS on reddit

138. When I think about it, boiling water for cooking and showers is the most fundamental process to sustain our modern society: The modern sophisticated world is basically dependent on digging the Earth to get resources to make fire (e.g., natural gas, oil, coal, etc).

139. According to my experience, there is a tipping point for every desire. Whatever it is, if you can endure until your craving passes, you just don't want it any more after that point.

140. Chicken must be the most beneficial dinosaur on earth. These birds (all of which are evolved from dinosaurs) eat ticks and insects – they produce fertilizers and proteins as a result.

141. "Animals eat other animals without any sauce or seasoning:" I think condiments are created to make people eat more, which is extremely detrimental for our health. Only restaurants and food producers make more money that way. I believe sugar is more harmful than salt and notice that Thai food includes sugars way more than others.

142. Korean and Thai foods are both nutritionally bad for our health (especially to teeth) in general, but Thai is definitely the worst in the world: Why? At least, *Kimchi* from Korea has probiotics and is beneficial for gut health. Korean food – minus Kimchi plus more sugar – is Thai food.

143. There was a popular *Korean book about Americans* titled "Sir Americans, Americans, Bastard Americans" written by Baik. In the book, he wrote that he had driven eight hours to eat

"Jjampong (Korean seafood soup)" in New Jersey once. In the middle, he confessed that he ended up settling in Korea for no profound reason – he just liked Korean food too much. You know what, though? He died of a heart attack at the age of 49 in 2010. Maybe he passed away because he was obese. Still, I believe Korean foods having extremely high salts (in general) didn't help his condition. I keep telling people that we should avoid Korean and Thai foods to be alive.

144. I haven't been interested in salad most of my life (45 years out of 50). I haven't ordered it as a single menu until recently. But, a couple of days ago, I felt a minor but obviously unpleasant pain in my teeth; I wondered if it's because of a lot of carbohydrate I had taken lately (from mostly pizzas and Banh mi sandwiches). Nonetheless, I was hungry, so I decided to try Sweet Green salad, which I haven't eaten for long due to their high prices. I remember I ate a little more salad with Cod fish oil dressing at home that night. You know what, though? The persistent *pain was completely gone* the next day! Not having tooth pain is priceless for me. I told my wife that I may have to eat only one bowl of salad a day when I am really old. Keeping my teeth and not having pain is more important than eating tasty foods to me. It also cleared kidney discomfort as well and I am sure I may have more of those symptoms from now on.

145. Before this happened, I was planning to visit "Paik's Noodle (Hong Kong Ban-jum)" once in my life. The place sells *Koreanized* Chinese foods (e.g., Champong, Chajang) and I know they include plenty of sugars or even caramels. But I thought I will try *just once*. That plan was canceled and I ate *garden salad* at Johnny's, which I am glad about. I don't feel any tooth pain now.

146. There is a group of Koreans who stick to only Korean foods. I notice that they usually cannot speak English well or not at all. I assume that the failure in food adaptation equals failures in language learning and cultural acceptance.

147. One of the reasons why I may have to keep staying in America is the healthy food. I can find salads literally everywhere in America (except Korean or Chinese restaurants). Even Thai restaurants have salad as a single menu item. But if I live in Korea, those harmful (Koreanized) Chinese restaurants become my default eateries. I have to search for salad in Korea, unless I make it myself. I will be getting old and *I like to stay away from pains,* which will be caused by wrong foods. Now I am eating other foods together with salad, but the salads could be my only foods near the end of my life. Besides, tastes are not necessarily bad, compared with other foods.

148. A tooth can rot under dental molding, onlay or crown. There is no way we can brush it with toothpaste, although I believe we can clean it by oil pulling (olive oil squishing) somehow. This is why it's important not to take any harmful food from the beginning, and drink only water.

149. Some Korean dentists estimate a natural tooth is worth $30,000 each. Don't damage it with $2 snacks.

150. "We think of things being alive or not, but there might be other states we can't conceive of." – pufballcat on reddit

151. When I was in a hair salon yesterday, I saw an old lady getting hair permed. The smell of her hair chemical was very bad and I believe very toxic, too. While I have never liked my curly hair particularly, I felt blessed since I don't have to go through such a thing, which even costs money on a regular basis. Likewise, we forget to realize how blessed we are in many cases.

152. Before I started writing as a profession, I thought the job is all about "writing well" – no, it's not and has never been. Surprisingly, *more than half is about marketing*, which is the reason why we see poorly written books all the time.

153. One of the privileges of being a nameless writer is I can write what I want. I cannot if I concern readers or winning an award.

154. "Your brain's job isn't to keep you happy, but keep you alive." – Anonymous

155. One person said "We run into a murderer at some point in our lives." I think one of the surest ways for men to run into a female criminal is going to a massage parlor. Again, sexual desire is the man's worst enemy.

156. To me, the biggest excitement has been my portfolio increase – not shopping, smoking, drinking or marijuana smoking. I have had the largest amount of joy in my life whenever I see my money growing. We make money since we need it. However, making money can be a pleasure, too – the biggest one, sometimes. I don't see *why not,* as we need money anyway.

157. Long term investment cannot be done only by patience. More importantly, we just need enough money to leave it alone for long. This is why most *people who invest with debt* lose.

158. Getting my money back (without a loss) is as important as making profit in investment.

159. Sell stocks when everyone talks about them. Usually, it's *the last stage* of price going up, when you detect the boom in reality.

160. One of the best ways to save a great amount of taxes *legally* is living in a small house. Property taxes are incredibly high, especially in America, and non-exemptible (or the least exemptible). It would be a large saving since we have to pay it every single year until we die.

161. Believe it or not, sometimes, we just don't need more money. We may *want* more out of comparison.

162. Personally, **Chase** bank did a lot of great things for me. I *lost* $1,000 in an ATM scam in 2009. Technically, it was not their fault, but Chase imbursed $1,000 to my account out of their pocket. Secondly, this JP morgan Chase made an ETF called JEPQ and it brings me a lot of profits now. I haven't invested in big tech companies (e.g., Google, Meta, Nvidia) until lately, since most of them don't have any dividends (personally, I buy only dividend stocks). Yet JEPQ gives me high dividends (9%) out of their own option trading, while investing in Nasdaq big techs, so I invested a good amount of money in it. In 2024, it is the #2 (second the most profitable) out of 107 positions in my portfolio. I

guess I will stay with them forever and try to benefit them in my own ways.

163. A report shows that surprisingly only one (1) Tesla vehicle was sold in South Korea in January 2024. This is shocking, although the automobile market is smaller there (totally, about 11,000 cars were sold nationally, including 9 Rolls-Royce and 7 Lamborghini cars). Simply, no one wants to buy a car making fire on its own and drivers cannot escape from it. Koreans are the smartest in that sense, but this would be a trend worldwide soon I believe. Nonetheless, I see a lot of people, especially Korean women, talk about buying more Tesla shares to average down, as its price went down a lot lately. To me, that is nonsense. In the coming next few quarters, Tesla sales and profit will obviously keep dropping. If anyone buys more TSLA, they only lose more money.

164. Being persistent in investing is easy: Just don't take a look at your portfolio often. You won't change anything, which equals "being consistent."

165. So far, I have avoided a lot of bad investments by choosing only (or mostly) dividend stocks. *I get dividends, regardless that the stock prices go up or down* – I get my profit, first. Then, I sell those stocks only when they go up, sometimes. This strategy looks simple, but it has worked out well for me.

166. I didn't watch the Super Bowl at all this year (every year, actually). I read that the lowest price for tickets on Sunday is $8,000 in 2024. It seems everyone watches the game, but I didn't check it out at all. Maybe I am not interested in American football.

Nonetheless, the important thing is not being swept by crowds – extremely crucial in investment.

167. I think America is a terrific country for stock investment, yet terrible for real estate investment; while it has a lot of great and massive corporations, property taxes on residence or other buildings are very high. This is why I don't really see a real estate mogul in America. Also, this is why most Americans, including the rich, have *only one house.*

168. On the contrary, South Korea is pretty much the opposite. While it doesn't have a huge company except Samsung, its property tax is 10 times cheaper than that of America. Even middle-class citizens have more than one house and having an extra rental income from it is common. In general, Koreans are very negative about stock investment (many think it's a gambling, which is true in a sense) and often they buy American stocks for dividend incomes.

169. Losing money can be the biggest pain and fear for some people. I watched a Tik Tok video from the police showing a Latina getting arrested for her 4th DUI in AZ. Ironically, my first question was, "How much fine does she have to pay?" The penalty is up to $25,000 and additional jail time, by the way.

170. As long as we live in the same house, there is no visible benefit out of "home value increase." In general, we only need to pay more property taxes (due to house price increase), while living in the same house.

171. In my particular case, actually there is an obvious advantage. I live in a condo complex (485 units total here) and I have to see less renters in this neighborhood that way. I have been a renter myself for 14 years in America and know that not all the renters are bad. Nonetheless, I notice that some renters make loud noises and cause troubles in this complex. Which is the reason why the board set up the rule that no one can rent their units, while the only owners can live in their units. But this rule has never been kept since many owners secretly have rented their units so far. The good news is that it may happen less, as unit prices go up here. Usually, investors buy a unit and rent it to others, only when it is cheaper. Financially, it doesn't make sense to do so (not profitable), when the property is expensive.

172. I bought my one-bedroom unit for $60,000 in 2013 (full cash). It's currently selling up to $180,000 now in 2024 and I expect it will be over $200,000 in 2025. I consider this a real estate *investment success.*

173. A little bit of patience makes a difference in stock investing, indeed. See if you can hold just one more day, week, month or year.

174. "The easiest way to attract beautiful women is to date another gorgeous one" – Anonymous

175. We don't have to envy people who have multiple partners. They may live in hell. Less is better. Having less relationships or no relationship at all is the best.

176. "Being ugly is very peaceful:" While I was working in the nursing home, I had so many unwanted approaches from female employees. The funny thing was that the ones I had been interested in never addressed me.

177. "We're more afraid of losing our jobs than dying:" I think people may perceive these two the same, since welfare has been invented only recently – there hasn't been any supporting system for most of *Sapiens'* 6 million years of history.

178. Stupidity always hurts others. Walking around Chicagoland is one of my favorite hobbies. When I walked along Wolf rd yesterday, I saw a Latino man (40) and his daughter (15) standing in front of a bus stop; usually, this is *a good sign* that *a bus is about to come.* These days, a lot of people check the bus schedule in advance, *especially with their smartphones,* and come right before the bus comes. Both had a smartphone in hand, anyway. So I stopped walking and decided to take the bus to the south for a while. But you know what? It never came and I wasted 40 minutes for nothing and had to walk away. Apparently, these two people, who I heard spoke in Spanish, use their phones only for entertainment (e.g., Tik tok, etc). *I didn't ask,* but it seems they don't know how to use Google to get info. When I glimpsed the girl's phone, a video was definitely on it. As a result, not only did they have to wait for long themselves, they wasted my time "without intention." In real life, being stupid is as bad as being evil, and it can hurt others.

179. While watching the movie *Oppenheimer,* I learned that all the physicists involved in the project were Jewish, starting from Einstein. Yuval Harari who wrote *Sapiens* (the smartest book I

have read) is also Jewish. I hate to admit this, but they might be the smartest people in the world.

180. Blacks are <u>not inferior</u>, contrary to what James Watson (Nobel prize winner) argued about. To me, Tupac is the reason why blacks are also smart; he (Tupac Amaru Shakur) basically invented a new genre of gangster rap, left the best songs (much better than the ones these days) and died at the age of 25 in 1996. I have thought that I am a smart guy, but I couldn't even write *one hit book* at the age of 50 now. I will try, but I am not even sure if I can do that in the next 50 years.

181. We need to wait until our bodies take enough rest and react.

182. Believe it or not, no one thinks about you all the time. People are interested in their own life.

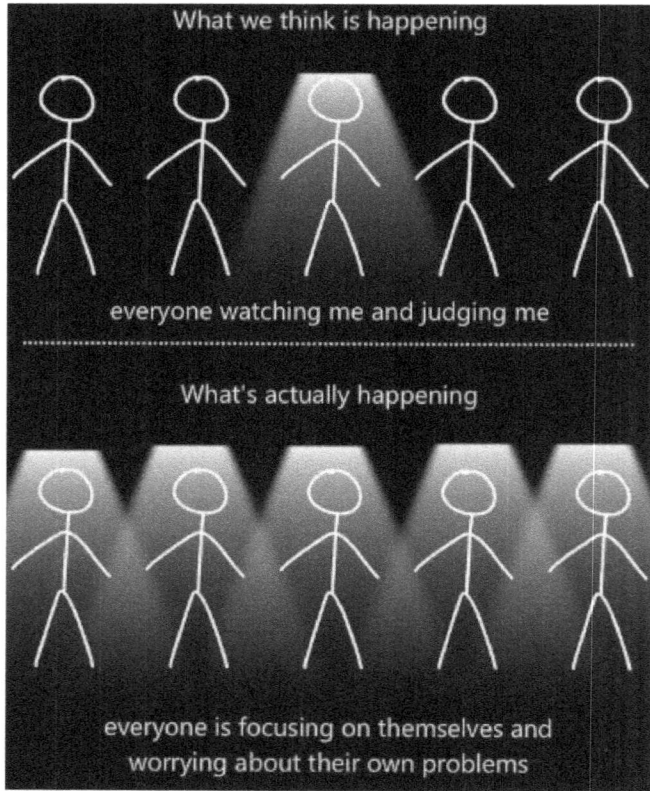

What we think is happening

everyone watching me and judging me

What's actually happening

everyone is focusing on themselves and worrying about their own problems

(image source: visualhustles on Instagram)

183. "The rich pay for premium subscriptions not to see ads for products they can afford, while the poor who can't afford it are forced to watch ads for things they can't pay:" This is true for YouTube subscriptions. Accidentally, I donated $10 to the Biden

campaign via its ad the other day, since I didn't want to see Trump on TV again. I personally don't own a TV and believe *the poor buy and watch TVs longer*, and go through more ads that way.

184. "The key to happiness is to always have something to look forward to." – Anonymous on Reddit

185. "The busiest person replies the quickest:" It's often untrue that he or she cannot reply since the person was too busy.

186. "The universe is 90 billion *light-years wide*, while the *maximum* speed known is *the speed of light*. If the Earth is the same size as the entire universe, this would be the same, if the maximum speed limit is around 0.5 micrometer/year."

187. "Being charged as an accessory is the crime version of a participation award." –Anonymous on Reddit

188. I notice that I check the internet more for fun when I am tired.

189. A perfect life happens only in the movies. Your life and relationships with others won't be perfect. And, that is OK – it is normal.

190. People who smile frequently are the true winners in our lives (not the ones who smile at the last moment, as in a movie).

191. "California has the most pedestrian-unfriendly cities, despite having the most pedestrian-friendly weather." – Anonymous on Reddit

192. I don't know why none of the cars has a solar panel on the roof generating power for the cars; certainly, we drive on sunny days. And I also have thought that the external unit of the air-con (condenser) should come with a solar panel to generate power for the unit. Why? We turn on the air-con usually on sunny days.

193. There is no incredible joy existing in our life. Having a lot of small but frequent joy is possible, though. Buying a $4 *kimchi mandu* (dumpling) at the Joongbu mark and walking along the Bloomingdale trail (The 606) was a great joy – it cost only $4 that day.

194. It seems committing suicide is increasing these days, especially in Korea. I think the right attitude is, "Why do I have to die now since we will be all dead, anyway." Apparently, we need a little bit of patience in everything. It's not like that "we live forever unless we kill ourselves."

195. When I watched "60 minutes" the other day, it showed a lot of Chinese crossing from Mexico into the U.S. at the Texas border in 2024 – it reported that they are the fastest growing ethnic group to transpass it illegally and some Chinese said they had to sell their houses to migrate to America that way (apparently, the international trip cost them a lot). A lot of Americans forget how lucky we are already – no reason to commit suicide in this country.

196. "When you're rich, your opinions carry weight even on matters you have no idea about." – Anonymous

197. When I checked the map, I realized that the country of Brazil is much nearer to the continent of Africa than I had thought. As a result, I heard there is a strong relationship between the Amazon forest and the Sahara desert. Experts said, "There is Amazon since there is Sahara."

198. Lazy people never really take vacations. Those people who take bold, frequent and obvious breaks are *usually* hard workers. People who have been burned out before don't hide their vacations.

199. Barack *Obama* is a true *outlier* in many senses. We all know that he is the first and only *black* president so far. On top of it, he became the president when he was just 47, which makes him the 5th youngest president out of 46 ones. Besides, he doesn't have a dirty scandal like Clinton or Trump, while those two are in the Epstein List.

200. It's not a bad idea to **take a rest in advance** before getting exhausted. Taking a rest doesn't mean spending money on entertainment. In fact, true rest comes *only when we don't spend money.*

201. There was a girl named Sarah in my previous job, which was a nursing home – a skinny Italian. I had been interested in her for a while, but had to let her go in the end. She was born and raised in America, but couldn't go to a college, although the community one here is pretty cheap. She was in her early 30s, but her face was severely damaged by too much drinking and smoking. I saw her car was crushed one day and thought, "that's it." There is no

obligation for me to go through obvious future miseries together. It was hard, but the right decision.

202. Most people intensively care about their appearances, although not many care for their voices.

203. One medical book suggested that there is the same amount of pleasure every human can experience during his or her lifetime. The doctor suggested that when we keep trying to lower our stimuli, we can be easily content by little joy.

204. Boredom can be the worst enemy generating troubles or formidable ground for productivity.

205. I spent 26 months completing my army service in Korea (November 1994 - January 1997). There was time that I thought it was a pure waste; then, I had to give away 26 months out of my 24 years of life. Now I don't feel like that any more at the age of 50 – it was a unique 2 years out of my boring 50 years. I guess it will be even more like this, as I grow older.

206. I watched some video clips about Palestinian and Ukrainian wars the other day. The worst enemy for a human is another human. No other animals will attack and kill humans like this. I am afraid humans will be exterminated by our own race in the end.

207. A large part of education is deception.

208. People who don't get deceived easily tend to *wander*.

209. We don't have to follow trends diligently to be a good investor. Actually, it's *the other way* around. We shouldn't care about the media too much – we need to move as reluctantly as possible.

210. "If you only read the books that everyone else is reading, you can only think what everyone else is thinking." –Haruki Murakami

211. When it comes to saving, I think we should take care of high expenses first – usually, these are housing and cars.

212. Humans always go for the most extreme. We don't go there all at once. We usually arrive there little by little and step by step, but *ultimately*.

213. Don't make yourself available all the time. That's one way to lower your value.

214. Mental maturation is the process of realizing that *material success is pointless*. Some people may end up disfavoring lavishness. In a sense, frugal people are more mature.

215. Most people fight and compete for more money or higher positions. Yet there are a few decent people who don't pursue those, despite their excellent qualities. Jean-Paul Sartre declined the Nobel Prize for Literature. Dr. Jonas Salk let go of his chance to make $billions out of patenting his polio vaccines. "Grand Prince Yang-nyeong" let go of his chance to be a king in Joseon and helped "Sejong the Great" to be the next monarch – Sejong eventually invented *Hangul*, so Koreans have used the letters for the last 500 years conveniently.

216. "In times of trouble, libraries are sanctuaries." – Susan Orlean

217. Some mature people choose "not being successful," intentionally. Some saints choose misfortune, instead of happiness.

218. Most people don't know this, but it shows that *the Sun is expanding slowly every year*. I was surprised that we didn't have much snow in Chicagoland this year in 2024. Surely, it's partly because of global warming. Simultaneously, I suspect we are getting close to the Sun by its expansion a little; according to scientists, the Earth will totally be burned out by the Sun five billion years later.

219. The Earth used to have the Ice ages, but we don't see it any more. We only see winters these days, which I believe are getting shorter gingerly. Which may be related to the Sun's gradual expansion.

220. Believe it or not, a lot of *fatal* infectious diseases has been originated from animals: cow (cowpox), chicken (chicken pox and avian flu), dog (measles and rabies), pig (swine flu), horse (typhus), lima (syphilis), monkey (AIDS), camel (MERS), bat (Covid), etc.

221. Out of those, syphilis and AIDS are venereal diseases (STDs). I wonder if some humans had sexual contact with limas and monkeys, originally. The rest are mostly contagious via air, though.

222. I assume contagions from animals may increase as the human population gets bigger – we keep invading their natural habitats more and will have new contacts with them.

223. Do you want to be remembered by others after you die? The best chance is writing a book. Kazuo Inamori was the founder of Japanese conglomerate Kyocera and died at the age of 90 in 2022. I learned about him as I ran into his book, "A Compass to Fulfillment" on Amazon. No one cares how rich he was when he was alive any more.

224. There are *three ways* to increase our *day time* and ultimately lifetime: Eating one meal a day, rising early and quitting browsing online. I believe we can get several extra hours a day this way. Most people don't realize it, but it takes hours to eat two more meals a day, which is unnecessary for our health.

225. After starting eating one meal a day for health reasons (only dinner), I notice that I eat *much slower* these days, too. It leads me to acting and speaking slowly as well – a slower way of doing other things step by step in general. Maybe this happens because I have some extra time for not eating two extra meals, which probably saves me a couple of hours every day. I can say that eating small has been a lifestyle changing experience rather than just a meal plan shift.

226. "*Today some 40 percent of us will discover we have cancer at some point in our lives.* Half of men over sixty and three-quarters over seventy, for instance, have prostate cancer at death without being aware of it. It has been suggested, in fact, that

if all men lived long enough, they would <u>all</u> get prostate cancer." – from "Body" by Bryson

227. Bill Bryson is a scientist and former chancellor of Durham University. The fact above is alarming since cancer can lead people to death in many cases. Apparently, one out of two old people get cancer before death. I am 50 this year, so I guess it's time for me to be concerned about this.

228. His book shows the major reasons to get cancer are drinking, smoking and eating too much (causing obesity). For now, I am glad that I haven't drank or smoked at all for life, although I believe I have eaten too much. I am skinny (125 pounds), but I believe I eat a lot *portion-wise*. I guess I didn't gain much weight due to frequent walking.

229. Here are two things I would like to try from now. First of all, I will eat garlic on a daily basis. Luckily, Korean foods have a lot of garlic and they eat them more than other people. Mount Sinai hospital explained that "In test tubes, garlic seems to kill cancer cells." Second is definitely eating one meal a day. Personally, I see that it takes at least 24 hours to digest all the food I eat (maybe even longer). I don't know who invented the "3 meals a day" concept in the beginning, but I would say it was a terrible creation – we only eat too much that way. The Mount Sinai site shows, "Cisplatin-resistant cancer cells are particularly susceptible to starvation-induced death."

230. Some may wonder why I got freaked out of getting cancer. My mother-in-law and cat died of liver and blood cancer, respectively. My cat was 17 years old, which was 87 in human age.

I saw his suffering very closely until his last day by euthanasia. Death by cancer is not peaceful – it's extremely painful, as countless pain relievers were invented solely for that, including morphine and fentanyl (opioid).

231. It seems a lot of people are not sure of their pets' age. Taking and having digital photos of my cat as soon as I adopted him were helpful.

232. Some people predict that paper books will disappear one way or another: *Wrong!* In my opinion, they will never disappear. Why? There is an eye disease called cataract, which forms a white fog in lenses in (usually) old people's eyes. One of the main causes is watching screens too long and often, including eBooks. Paper books never really cause this problem and are much safer for the eyes.

233. No one can win against a person who doesn't have a desire. *Wanting something* can be our <u>biggest weakness.</u>

234. We are looking and experiencing miracles everyday. The true *miracle* happened here on Earth *when a life formed.*

235. Happiness is a *relative* feeling. In fact, there is no absolute or continuous one. People tend to feel happy as long as their situation is *better than others.*

236. I think the best weapons to collapse the North Korean regime are the TVs and internet, especially from South Korea. South Koreans already call North Korean refugees "new friends in town" and give monthly minimum incomes to support them. Some

South Koreans complain about "tax spending" on their incomes, but I think we should consider it as military spending rather than welfare support – it's cheaper than having a war against North Korea.

237. *Less than half of all women are marriable.* Which is the reason why high divorces are everywhere.

238. When we start a business, I think it's better to focus on helping others than making money. By accident, I visited a restaurant named "The best cutlet (tonkatsu)" in Chicagoland the other day. I walked away after checking their menus on the kiosk machine since meals started from $15 for a basic cutlet (I know that no one charges that much for the menu in general). Later, I learned that it's a franchise cafe from Korea – *known for "$7 cutlets"* in the country. I think the original founder started it to help students enjoy their meals at low cost. Then, the Korean American owner brought it here solely to make money. I felt it's *too greedy* to charge *more than double* for the same menu. No wonder why the restaurant was *completely empty* when I was there.

239. I decided to give up making money out of selling books – basically, they are my gifts to people. Nonetheless, writing will be my way to relieve stress and cure depression. I believe I already make more than enough out of investment each year. And, ironically, I believe this mindset is the way I can continue writing persistently until I can make some sales in the end.

240. So far, countless people have downloaded my books for free, but less than ten people bought my paperbacks (I truly appreciate

them). I have 33 followers in my Amazon account, as of March 2024. I think my books are just *not good enough* that people want to spend money on them yet.

241. My wife mentioned that the diet drug, Ozempic, costs $900 for a one-month supply (2024). I cannot believe people spend money even on losing weight. Not eating should be more than enough, which is actually the only way, after all. Besides, honestly, I don't believe the drug is safe for our bodies.

242. I walked with my daughter the whole day yesterday. Don't waste your time at the gym. Walking instead of driving and hauling some groceries in the backpack on the way back has worked out for me (*125 pounds* at 5' 7").

243. Taking care of a child is endless work, even after he or she becomes an adult.

244. I will never do option trading for one simple reason: Our price predictions always can go wrong: Why? When we make a prediction, it always includes *our wishes.* But reality works *on its own,* independently.

245. The stocks I strongly suggest not to touch are Tesla, and any ETF related to Bitcoin or any type of coin (2024). I already wrote two books regarding TSLA and believe tons of people will lose money by it.

246. I am 50 this year and have forgotten that there was time I could try everything without worrying about money. I didn't have

to support anyone, consistently like this. I think we can live freely only for the first 30 years of our lives.

247. People who look for material success and wealth too much are mentally *immature* ones. It's understandable to do so when we are relatively young, but it's a shame to keep doing that after we get older. In fact, people often get blinded by greed and lose more after certain points unnecessarily.

248. There is a limited amount of tasks anyone can achieve _alone_. Still, I prefer working alone than making more money by teaming with others. Handling other people has been stressful for me for life. I am glad I have accumulated enough savings, so I am not forced to do *what I hate*.

249. Reading books brings us more money. I notice that the net worth of Microsoft is the biggest in the world back again in 2024. *Bill Gates* is known to *read a lot*.

250. If you don't know what to do to be wealthy, just throw out your smartphone and start reading books.

251. "Libraries are everyman's free university." – John Jake

252. Yesterday, the stock market crashed, but my portfolio has been up. *There is why I have bought more than enough bonds* (65% of my portfolio). Bonds provide good monthly income (up to 19% interest in case of TLTW). More importantly, they protect the whole portfolio against loss, due to stock market crashes.

$585,043.53
+$813.90 (+0.14%) Today's Gain/Loss

$587.5K

$463.8K

$340.2K

1M   YTD   1Y   3Y

U.S. markets closed.

DJIA	NASDAQ	S&P 500
39,475.90	16,428.82	5,234.18
-305.47 (-0.77%)	+26.98 (+0.16%)	-7.35 (-0.14%)

F 11A 1P 3P   F 11A 1P 3P   F 11A 1P 3P

Crude Oil	Gold	US 10 Year	Bitcoin
80.82 -0.31%	2,166.50 -0.83%	42.18 -1.24%	64,553.00
			+1.58%

Crude Oil and Gold delayed 10 mins

253. I made over $63,000 profit out of investment last year (2023). Financial knowledge will be more important than anything else (e.g., jobs, business ownership, etc) in wealth building from now on.

1i	
1h	
1z	
2b	6,988.
est	
3b	22,895.
dends	
4b	
unt	
5b	
unt	
6b	
unt	
7	33,705.
8	53.
9	63,□1.
10	0.
11	63,□1.
12	
13	505.
14	
15	42,□6.

ome

11320B

Form 1040 (2023)

254. Some people get extreme joy out of saving money and accumulating wealth – they are happy when they see their portfolio increased whenever they log into their accounts in the morning.

255. A lot of people just focus on making more money in the stock market. Nonetheless, I believe "not losing" is more important, especially when we deal with a large amount of capital. We will get wealthy in the end, if we don't lose anything,

256. Nothing happens in the stock market for most days of the year. Statistically, I heard something happens for only about 15 days a year. But those who are addicted to trading try to make something happen unnecessarily (they usually try some option or short term trading before closing). That's when *financial tragedy* happens. **People mostly lose money by hurrying a profit to come out of nowhere.**

257. To me, the stock market success came with *passing many boring days pointlessly, while getting dividends.* Some call people like me a "patient investor" – the fact is that I am not patient at all. I am just not addicted to quick profits.

258. *Leaving a portfolio alone* is a way to make money. *Don't check it everyday.* I think I will check it for only 10 minutes a day to transfer dividends to my bank account every morning.

259. Profit realization (selling stocks with profits) is *always right.* **If you are wondering** if you have to sell a stock or not, **just sell**

it, *if it brings you a profit.* There is a reason why you are wondering – *get rid of a headache!*

260. Now I have 25 ETFs, 47 company stocks and 38 company bonds in my portfolio, as of March 2024 – totally, 110 positions. Nothing happens most days. It seems I have to wait for long to sell at least 12 stock positions with profits, as interest is expected to go down eventually.

261. Believe it or not, getting dividends and interests is very addictive and I notice that I am eager for more everyday. There was a time that I felt 6% dividend from Pfizer stock was enough. Soon after that, JEPI and JEPQ giving 10% dividends have been my two biggest positions. Lately, I have bought TLTW giving 19% dividend and I am starting to touch TSLY giving a surprising 80% dividend a year now.

SCHV	$74.0893	+$0.20	+$8.40
SCHWAB US LARGE-CAP V...	+$0.2093	+0.28%	+12.80%
SPYD	$39.96	+$23.00	+$443.66
SPDR PORTFOLIO S&P 500 ...	+$0.23	+0.57%	+12.48%
JEPQ	$53.66	+$135.00	+$4,946.50
J P MORGAN EXCHANGE T...	+$0.15	+0.28%	+11.41%
SCHD	$78.74	-$0.10	+$39.03
SCHWAB US DIVIDEND EQ...	-$0.02	-0.03%	+11.00%
BBEU	$59.365	+$0.07	+$5.36
J P MORGAN EXCHANGE T...	+$0.075	+0.12%	+9.93%
HDV	$106.98	+$2.55	+$125.68
ISHARES CORE HIGH DIVI...	+$0.17	+0.15%	+8.49%
SCHB	$60.39	+$1.55	+$18.78
SCHWAB US BROAD MARK...	+$0.31	+0.51%	+6.63%
VYM	$117.69	+$0.35	+$35.54
VANGUARD WHITEHALL F...	+$0.07	+0.05%	+6.42%
FENY	$24.13	+$18.00	+$386.28
FIDELITY MSCI ENERGY IN...	+$0.06	+0.24%	+5.63%
VCLT	$78.4299	+$56.97	+$916.15
VANGUARD SCOTTSDALE ...	+$0.1899	+0.24%	+4.05%
BBHY	$46.0599	+$41.97	+$533.39
J P MORGAN EXCHANGE T...	+$0.1399	+0.30%	+4.01%
JEPI	$57.035	-$94.50	+$1,748.64
J P MORGAN EXCHANGE T...	-$0.105	-0.19%	+3.52%
VTIP	$47.875	+$15.00	-$22.50
VANGUARD SHT-TERM INF...	+$0.075	+0.15%	-0.24%
TSLY	$16.06	-$4.45	-$5.70
TIDAL TR II YIELDMAX TSL...	-$0.09	-0.62%	-0.79%
TLTW	$26.655	+$16.95	-$810.18
ISHARES TR 20+ YEAR TR ...	+$0.015	+0.05%	-2.62%

262. In a sense, I am glad I have been crazy about only dividends. As I said, humans tend to end up being in the most extreme situations for one way or another. As Tesla stock has been down a lot lately (March 2024), I decided to start buying TSLY etf, which they said gives a 80% dividend a year via *synthetic covered call strategy*. If I have been crazy about capital gain, all my money could have gone through option trading already. I don't think my money will be gone via more dividends – at least, not all of them as *in the case of options*.

263. I bought 50 shares of TSLY last week. Today I sold it all with a profit. For some reason, a Tesla stock or related ETF, which is TSLY in this case, always gives me worry whenever I own it; their volatilities are high. A crazy 80% dividend sounds attractive, but I decided to let it go for my peace of mind.

264. I actually bought 170 shares of TSLY again at $15.69 today. These are supposed to bring me probably $300 extra dividend a month.

265. After consideration, I decided to sell out all of my TSLY shares again. I cannot explain, but something is not right about this specific investment. Besides, I don't really like the original company Tesla, anyway.

266. The worst part of TSLY is NAV (my original money invested) gets smaller, while getting dividend (TSLY had a reverse split already, although it's not even two year old). Imagine your savings get smaller in the bank, while you get interest every month. It's

not even saving in that case – you just get your money back, which doesn't make sense.

267. Worrying makes us not do anything. I couldn't write anything while I was holding TSLY stock for the last two weeks.

268. My nervousness about TSLA and TSLY stock was from the fact that I cannot trust its CEO Elon Musk. He is not the type of a person I can hand my money over to do a business together. I don't deal with drug addicts as my business partner.

269. Investing while having debt worry doesn't make sense. Remember: We make money to be happy.

270. Selling with profit is always right in stock trading.

271. Personally, I don't buy or trade coins at all. When Bitcoin ETFs were approved by the SEC in January 2024, I bought 20 shares of FBTC. Its price dropped a lot as soon as I bought it and I spent a miserable 2 weeks suffering under the loss; then it went up, so I sold them all with $8 profit quickly – that's all. I know *coins can drop any time and there is no real ground to support their prices.*

272. Getting rid of a debt is lowering risk in finance – it is always the right movement.

273. Some *losers choose gambling,* even when they can invest.

274. There are two ways to make money out of the stock market. One is the traditional way – buying a stock of a profitable company

– we all know it. The other way is to make money out of other investors. Sometimes, the mass investors make a mistake altogether at the same time. If you bet against them or not do what they do, you can make money, too. This is why it's important that you shouldn't be drowned in the major trend.

275. "India accounted for 78% of all options in 2023 and 95% of those were only held for less than 30 minutes with *only 10% of them making money*." – Axis News

276. I usually don't do what most people do, especially in the stock market.

277. I don't think I will spend a lot of money from now. I like to read all the books in the world – all the books in our library, at least!

278. I don't think my books include a lot of love emotions: Why? Maybe I don't want to suffer from them again.

279. There are two main reasons why I write books. First, I like to be remembered. Second, I like to show you how awesome a person I am.

280. Things to write about are already with us – we just cannot see them since these are too close.

281. There is a Latina (Mexicana) writer named Erika. While I read her book (a sort of autobiography), I learned she married a divorced man who already has two children from his previous marriage before meeting her. That reminded me of the singer

Park who I mentioned in *UnBrokable** series before. To me, that's a *loss* already since she was single without having a child, then: Why would a young single girl marry an old man having two kids from another woman? She eventually has a daughter with him, so he has to support three children now. I met my wife 25 years ago when she was 23; not only was she single, but a virgin, too; we have one daughter together.

282. There was a girl named Ariana when I was working at the nursing home before quitting in 2022. She was only 19, but fat at that time. I checked her photo online lately and found she looks so much different from who I remember (in a *negative* way). She was supposed to be 21, but looked like 35. I am glad I can easily forget her or I don't have to wonder if I had to address her or not back then. When she becomes 30, I will be 59. I know she was into an old man, so let me see if she stays unmarried until then.

283. Some say people are the happiest in their 50s. I am 50 this year and occasionally feel that it could be true. I used to have a lot of worries, but most of the problems have been solved now. I don't have to worry about college graduation or mandatory army service completion (in Korea) any more. I bought my house 12 years ago and have lived without a car for 6 years now. I met my wife 25 years ago and we have a daughter, who is 14 already. I feel I have less and less things to worry about everyday.

284. One of the blessings from getting old is having lower sexual desire, to be honest. A lot of people falsely believe that having more libido and sexual encounters are good things: *Wrong!* Personally, I have a child already; *unless we want more children, technically, the desire is frequently a curse.* There are countless

people who died of AIDS or live with HIV currently, including celebrities. People living with HIV can be dead any time, often painfully. I would rather live my life without that kind of worry. Blissfully, I just don't feel a strong urge any more and I believe it has been like this since I was 45 (nonetheless, less and less every year).

285. Becoming a mother means getting into the world of poop. Being an adult means being responsible for cleaning a lot of dirty things.

286. There were times I had always felt masturbation was not enough and been willing to spend a chunk of money to meet a girl. It's not like that I don't want it completely, but luckily I just don't have an extreme urge any more. Just masturbating once a week or so has been fine in the last few years and that has been less and less as time went by. Personally, I just don't understand why some old people get charged with sexual crimes, including solicitation. It's not like I try to be a moral person, but I assume having less desire is the natural way of getting old.

287. Today I went to Vogelei park in Hoffman Estate. I remember it had like 10,000 fishes in its small pond last summer. Surprisingly, it didn't have anything at all (no animal or plant in the pond) this spring; I believe that it just had an annual clean up. I cannot believe *that many* fishes were created every year.

288. Internet trolls tackle little things. They are not interested in learning and growing themselves.

289. Every drug addict deserves death. I believe it's too much to waste the 911 emergency crews to save them. They made a choice, so we should let them go with it.

290. "The story is truly finished, not when the author adds the last period, but when the reader enters." – Celeste NG

291. What makes a person more attractive? In common, I think we feel attraction from skinny people.

292. I am reading a novel written by a Korean female writer – *The girl breadwinner in the house*. She wrote that she bought her family house with her name, instead of her parents. She didn't mention that she did it with a massive mortgage until the end, which was not exactly buying or owning a house.

293. Some people lose money since they are too diligent.

294. Don't trust anyone, including your parents and governments.

295. I saw a young girl's photo taken in Auschwitz during WWII the other day. I was shocked. The feeling is totally different after I have my own daughter.

296. ISIS-K terrorists from Afghanistan attacked a Russian concert hall and killed 133 people the other day in March 2024. I initially thought they were from Ukraine, but feel Russia has too many different enemies everywhere.

297. More profit is not important – less risk is. This is true, especially when we have a lot of money to handle.

298. Poor people have more *deadlines*. Being wealthy means having *less small deadlines*, stresses and pressures.

299. "A poem is never finished, only abandoned." – Paul Valery

300. This means we cannot make a perfect book, but need to let go of the manuscript we are working on at a point. It will be published after we *give up* working on it longer.

301. We blame people who spend a lot. We call people spending more than they can afford irresponsible. However, we rarely criticize those who have more children than they can afford.

302. Please do not encourage overbreeding. In the worst case, it can eventually kill us all in the end. We don't have another Earth to provide more resources to everyone.

303. I spoke with my previous coworker the other day and he said the notorious sous-chef Carlos is finally gone from the kitchen; he said, "Everyone is good now." I still cannot get back to the job since anyone horrible can come in there anytime.

304. Our prejudices hardly change. People still think cooking is for women, while most professional chefs and restaurateurs are men.

305. It was proposed that our smartphones actually listen to our conversations and use the info to make money. I think that's technologically possible.

306. We don't have to be available to others all the time.

307. There is nothing wrong with living paycheck to paycheck – humans have lived like that for millions of years. While I don't live like that, I feel the finance industry tries to make money out of painting it as a problem.

308. Drinking and smoking is not an act of enjoyment. If you truly think so, you are brain damaged.

309. I say this in the morning about once a year: "Today is the first day of the rest of my life." It would be great if I can say this once a month or week.

310. Married men should spend time with their children and family first. I see some spend most of their time with their friends, acquaintances or other women – results are never good.

311. I need to help myself and my family before helping others. Being selfish is the reason why an animal is surviving.

312. There are three types of intelligence: logical, emotional and social. All of these are important.

313, Although the Covid era seems to be over, I still wear a mask whenever I am indoors. There are a couple of advantages. First of all, I don't have to show my face; I hate that some people recognize me when I try to be private. Secondly, it actually helps me not catch all types of colds, including COVID, occasionally.

314. Most entertainments has been created to help us forget about deaths – the fact that we die someday.

315. Dating is one of the efforts to let us leave an offspring before we die. It's nonsense to discourage it.

316. Becoming an underaged parent is a concept created only recently. It's perfectly natural that an animal tries to breed before it passes away. I became a parent when I was 37, though.

317. I have become 51 this year. Sometimes, I truly wonder what has been *the meaning of my life*. More importantly, did I contribute anything on Earth yet?

318. My answer above is *definitely no* – not particularly. Maybe I produced "one human being" with my wife. Possibly, my daughter can do something good for everyone on Earth later on. I have consumed a lot of things to be alive (e.g., foods and resources) in the last five decades like other humans - that's about it. I didn't do anything beneficial in particular.

319. At the same time, maybe I didn't do anything noticeably invasive, either.

320. I still remember I caught little green frogs when I was about 10 in the countryside in Korea; it was summer time. I put them in a milk cartoon, so I could carry them home – my plan was watching them grow at home. I remember I found all of them dead half an hour later. If I didn't exist, could they live a little longer? *Again, I don't remember if I have contributed anything.*

321. These days, I write every day. I just feel so empty that I waste the day if I don't.

322. I realize that I don't feel any satisfaction from watching movies any more. I watch *"short* YouTube videos" all the time, though. I guess this will be the trend from now.

323. I honestly don't know why Taylor Swift is popular. I have never liked her songs. She seems to be too big and old to look cute, so I don't know what the stadiumful of cheering is about.

324. Maybe one sacrifice I made was the Korean army service of 26 months and 2 weeks, so far. I am glad I helped one young soldier who was apparently singled out and discriminated against – I bought him a few snacks to eat and listened to his troubles for an hour. I gave him a good dinner time. I am glad I did it before graduating the service.

325. There is no bad experience, after all – we need *both* failure and success to get better.

326. We don't have to be stingy not to click "like" on others' Instagram posts. I click on others all the time, but not many seem to do it on mine.

327. Try everything as long as you don't get into debt. Don't start an investment or business with debt.

328. To me, the first step to solve a problem is writing it down. Usually, it's a couple of simple sentences. It helps see the issue from a different angle.

329. While I worked at the nursing home, what I hated the most was the lunch breaks. I hated going back to work from it, while I was full, so I skipped eating occasionally. Now I am much happier, not being employed.

330. Personally, I cannot do two things at the same time. When I try, the results are always worse.

331. Instinctively, *men prefer a young girl (even if she is broke) to a rich old woman.* They can choose a wealthy old lady, but I would say that's probably going against their instincts.

332. We don't make every decision based solely on instincts.

333. A person's true character and quality come out, when things go wrong. This is why it's important to take a trip with your partner before marriage. Something always goes wrong while traveling.

334. Often, praising myself costs patiences of others.

335. If you want to improve your relationship with your partner, start with closing your mouth. Stop making unnecessary noise.

336. Lately, a Korean professor named Keum, who was also Miss Korea beauty pageant winner in 2002, has been on the news all over Korea – she married a senior man, who is 26 years older than her. I have seen the similar in my previous work, too. To make a long story short, apparently, it seems *about 10% of women truly dream of a much older man as a partner.*

337. Most people like to talk rather than listen. By being willing to listen, we can make a lot of friends.

338. We don't have to exaggerate or advertise our own success – people know it for one way or another via communication.

339. Never inform your success by your own mouth. When others find it out coincidently, it's much more effective. We can keep decency that way.

340. Most people don't remember what they ate for breakfast or a new person they met yesterday. Most of us just pass one day and another pointlessly, which is fine.

341. No one cares much about you, unless you are another Swift. Don't get into debt to look fancy (e.g., loan for a luxury car). Seriously, sometimes, it seems some people study, "How can I lose more money?"

342. Please trust me that I like to have good relationships with my parents. But there are a few things I will never understand among what they did. For those reasons, I really don't want to speak with them any more.

343. What I didn't like about my mother is she always looked at me with greed – it's more clear after I have my own daughter. I don't push my child to get better grades. Maybe I don't trust the modern educational system. More importantly, above all, there is no reason for me to do so.

344. One way to promote your books on Amazon KDP is not through paid advertisements. Just write more books and provide more free e-copies through the 5-day promotions; it brought me more Kindle page readings, income, recognition and reviews. It seems this is how the KDP algorithm works.

345. The second best way to promote is to make "A+ contents pages" for all the books and fill them up.

346. There are two things we need to be a good writer: plenty of micro experiences and *some time not doing anything.* **People tend to be creative, when they don't do anything.**

347. Ironically, people focus on being busy, instead of being relaxed or peaceful these days. The bottom reason for that is loneliness. *People get busier to get out of feeling isolated and empty.*

348. The bad part of saving money is that we may not spend it all before we die. *The worst part* is that it can be inherited by someone who can waste it all.

349. Don't just save money blindly. Spend some yourself, when there is a need.

350. Most people don't realize this, but *living longer is a sort of win.* I feel that whenever I check Wikipedia. People who die early by imprudent accidents are losers.

351. To me, anyone leaving a legacy is a winner. Most people don't leave a book or music - many just focus on making money (more) and die one day. No one will remember you unless you leave something – especially a thing people can read or listen to.

352. I heard that new trends usually come in literature first. Then, it spreads to art (paintings) and finally to music.

353. Passionate love is not necessarily a better or pure one – often it consists of greed, prejudice and nasty ownership. Trying to own a person always makes him or her an enemy.

354. Greedy love never turns out fine. Even if it does, it doesn't give a fulfillment to anyone – those lovers will be still unsatisfied.

355. Rarely, I see some love graffiti on a tree or on cement of pedestrian pavement (e.g., J LOVE K). Why do people do this? Love is an unstable emotion; I guess some want to make it fixed and permanent that way.

356. In a view, freedom and solitude are the same thing.

357. Everyone believes there is something they can do better than others – which is true in a sense. Try to recognize what that is. Or pretend you found that out. The person will be yours.

358. There is something we can learn from others. I notice that my daughter is getting along with others very well. It's something I need to learn from her.

359. Praising others, instead of praising yourself – you will make more money by it.

360. *When interacting with others, make them feel accepted and respected* – Dale Carnegie believed this as the most important life rule.

361. If you own a small store type of business, make sure of one thing – you may not be extremely smart (I wasn't, at least). To tell

the truth, if you are clever businesswise, you wouldn't be just a store owner. Regardless, when I was at a Subway on Barrington the other day, the Indian owner changed the register menu a little bit to trick me into paying $4 more: How could he think I didn't catch it?

362. In a sense, all human beings are merely renters on Earth; we just rent for 80 years or so and pass away.

363. Being famous costs a lot; it interrupts our personal lives any time, often intrusively.

364. I used to update my Facebook account everyday. When I was in Ikea one day, suddenly the cashier boy recognized who I was and said he followed my FB. Suddenly, I realized that there were so many people knowing me through the site (more than I could ever imagine). That was the day I decided to stop updating it.

365. Having negative experiences and feelings are perfectly normal – *inevitable* as long as we are alive.

366. Acting broke may keep us wealthy – ignore others!

367. A mistake repeated more than <u>twice</u> may actually be considered a *decision.*

368. Being in peace costs us money – *a lot*, sometimes.

369. Don't try to do things very well. Instead, <u>just do it</u>. Often doing average is more than enough.

370. The failure after doing our best is a success.

371. There is selfishness, jealousy and sexual desire on the bottom of our hearts – the foundations. Knowing this helps us understand human behaviors better.

372. Being old doesn't mean being mature. I found this out, only after I got old myself.

373. My daughter is 37 years younger than me. There is something I need to learn from her and also the actress IU – they seem to get along with others very well. She always plays nice with others.

374. The most formidable enemy anyone can meet is the one who visits bookstores and libraries – the one who reads all the time.

375. I have been a full time author in the past two years, but I have not been successful yet. Then, at least, I think I should be "the most failed writer in history," *instead* – the writer who wrote a large amount of books, yet failed.

376. People are drawn to a tragic story. That's why we are fascinated by the life story of Gogh. I think I can create one for myself like him.

377. The secret to writing a large amount of articles is persistence formed by habit. I start writing as soon as I wake up and don't do anything else until I finish one chapter or so.

378. Soju must be the most popular alcohol drink in South Korea now. Yet believe it or not, it's not even a proper drink. It's a mere industrial chemical consisting of ethanol and sweetener; both of which are particularly detrimental to teeth. Popularity of this drink is the reason why Koreans have the highest cancer mortality rate among the men in their 40s.

379. In general, Koreans are strangely generous about alcohol consumption. Oddly, they promote or even force it on others to drink. While I personally don't drink or smoke at all, garbage students actually encourage drinking in my college in Korea.

380. The best way to grow *inner power* is reading. Stop browsing the internet (including social media). Start living your real life by turning it off.

381. Do you know how to attract a girl? Just listen to her. *She must revisit you.*

382. I watched the Korean drama "My mister" starring an actress named IU the other day. Her angry, but calming character (as a poor girl in the drama) was impressive. I like a girl who knows some of the dark sides of our lives.

383. However, I learned that *her real life* is very different from the movie – a very successful young singer living in a $10 M condo. I suddenly didn't feel attraction from her. Weirdly, she looked pretty when she looked desperate and upset (to me).

384. FYI, this actress IU doesn't own a car or even a driver's license. I live without a car myself, although I have had a driver's license for the last 25 years.

385. Korean celebrity IU has donated a lot in the last 15 years (people estimated the accumulated amount is 10 M). I also respect her since she has become a topstar without using the "concept of sexy."

386. There is one thing common between my wife and IU – they give and donate. I am glad I met this type of person for my family. She will save my life some day.

387. Still, drama is just drama. The more I watch "My mister," it shows more nonsense.

388. Romance scams are real. When I was on Instagram, surprisingly, IU spoke to me herself and wondered if I could buy her concert ticket for $500. I blocked the scammer – whoever that was – but it was more tempting than I had ever expected.

389. Pay all the debt first before starting investing. Peace of mind is more important than anything else, including profit. Worrying causes an emotional cost, which is huge.

390. Possibly another success? The new Tesla earnings report is coming, so I bought 1,000 shares of TSDD, which is 2X inverse of TSLA. I expect I will make more than $1,000 out of this, as this stock is *90% hopium*[1].

---

[1] Hope + opium.

391. Unfortunately, this plan has not been successful yet, as of May 2024. It seems I have to wait for a couple of months to get my money back in July 2024. Regardless, the company is in a bad shape and its stock "TSLA" has terrible ratings.

392. The CEO Musk asks for a $58 billion pay package this year (2024); the decision will be made in June 2024. Some CEOs work for free or some companies buy back their stocks, when things are not in order. All Elon wants is money (eat and run) from the company, despite Tesla's latest troubles and layoffs. For now, I am glad I bought the reverse stock for TSLA.

393. I am curious what would happen after stock dilution by Musk, as a 58 B he asks is big.

394. I am waiting, but I assume TSLA won't go down deep before Robotaxi release in August this year (2024).

395. As I mentioned in my book, the direction of Tesla's business is wrong. No one wants FSD, as some actually enjoy driving. They should have taken care of electrical fire problems first.

396. Waymo from Google plans to launch a Driverless car as well (2024). They are using cars from the Jaguar brand now.

397. Apparently, Teslams (Tesla stock supporters) use everything to pump up TSLA prices now.

398. I decided to write without ambition from now on. I just don't want to pass a day without doing anything.

399. I think Italians must be the proudest. The Roman alphabet, which was invented 2,700 years ago, has been the most universally used in the world. Their main dishes, pizza and pasta, have conquered the dinner tables throughout the nations.

400. There is a black female writer named Destiny Harris. She has written over 1,400 books, when I checked it last time (2024). Today I found out that there are only 4 books on her Amazon author page. I don't know what happened suddenly, as she doesn't answer my email.

401.   There is no true love between man and woman – it always comes with conditions like beauty or money.

402.   Chris Smith was the most stupid human being I have ever seen – the owner of the Jazzercise next door, while I had my business in 2013. She didn't make any money, although made a lot of noise out of the old aerobics; she was already 50 years old then. I honestly think that's too old age to make that kind of mistake.

403.   Sugar and internet addictions are two enemies I need to fight until I die.

404.   Being unknown is a blessing. Most don't realize it until they lose privacy.

405.   We don't have to be famous – living unknown is perfectly fine. Actually, in animal survival, hiding is critical. So those people trying to get known actually go against our instincts.

406.   Our memories are strange. There was an obese filipina in my previous job. No matter how I tried, I couldn't remember her name. Nonetheless, now I do. Sometimes, it takes a few days to remember it.

407.   What I need the most is decency. I turned 51 last month and realized that that's what I need the most.   It can save my life in the best case.

408.   I like girls who are reasonably tall. I don't know why, but a considerable amount of girls, even for young ones, are short these days. Heights are mostly genetic, though.

409.   The internet is a sort of opium interrupting my life on a daily basis.

410.   Believe it or not, all I need is an incredible amount of time and boredom. I will start reading to get out of it and writing, subsequently.

411.   Single guys are winners only until 40. After 50, married men with their own families are winners.

412.   Debt happens when the poor try to spend more.

413.   In Korea, the slang "became a star" means "passed away." Also, "made an *extreme choice*" means "committed a suicide."

414.   There are only two things I will ask my daughter: a reading habit and "no drinking and smoking." It's OK if she (14) doesn't get good grades. Except for those two, the rest are at her own discretion.

415.   Just buy ETFs, instead of individual stocks or bonds.

416.   We don't need 10 M to retire completely. To me, $600,000 has been enough, although I believe it will grow in the next 50 years.

417.   Porsche is not a safe car at all. Don't assume it comes with good safety features, only because it's super expensive.

418.   There is no extraordinary reason to get divorce: Simply, assholes divorce more. I know if a person is divorced or not, or how many times, after 30 minutes' talk with him or her.

419.   If you don't know which women you need to marry, just choose the one with the highest education. My daughter studies crazily these days and I know it's from my wife.

420.   The enemy of immersion is desire for success – may be "greed" in a sense.

421.   I enjoy writing. But I am often discouraged by those numbers of social media followers or reviews from Amazon. Let me tell you a story about frustration.

422.   This girl lives in a $10 M house (she is a singer and actress in Korea). She is believed to have donated $10 M in the last 15 years; people estimate her net worth is over $100 M.

423.　However, did you know that she failed her music audition at least 20 times over the course of 3 years? It seems she lost the count in the end.

424.　On top of it, she also mentioned that she lost a large amount of money by fraud broadcasting brokers.

425.　Besides, her first two albums (29 songs) seem to be disastrous. Personally, I have never heard of any of them, although I started recognizing her songs from her 3rd album.

426.　What would have happened to me if I were in her shoes? Probably I would have given up completely after 5 auditions or so.

427.　In real life, I didn't have courage to apply even for one audition. Maybe that's why she is there and I am here now.

428.　Frankly, I am not totally broke, either. Nonetheless, I am glad I happened to like one of her characters in a drama (not the real person). Among all the girls I like, she is the second one who is wealthier than me.

429.　Human greed has no limit. There is no way we can fulfill them.

430.　Elon Musk is asking for another $56 billion now, although he already has $209 billion. Likewise, more likely, I will never be happy with any amount of money I will have in the future.

431.   Time to give up is for getting more – Or instead, I can drive my greed into different things.

432.   For example, I like to write as many books as possible. Or I will read and review more books, which will bring me more readers in the end.

433.   There is no way we can fulfill our sexual desires.

434.   Just let it go. Money will at least help me economically one way or another. Sexual desire won't help anything.

435.   I don't have a plan to take care of another baby, to begin with. However, it can also bring me HIV, STD, violence, divorce, charges, etc.

436.   Let your desire pass – don't try diligently to fulfill it.

437.   Every desire has a limit – no desire stays forever.

438.   "People's fingerprints are unique. As 8 billion fingerprints are all different, if we can identify one, we know who it belongs to, accurately. How come everyone's situation, inside story or thought can be the same, considering all the fingerprints are different? Nonetheless, we often act as if we know everything about the others."

439.   "Whatever goal you accomplished, somebody has helped you."

440.   Lecture of a successful Korean CEO: "Whenever I win a big contract or surprising sales, I submerge myself with a few books for a while. If I meet people too early, I may show arrogance to them, subconsciously. I try to calm myself down, reading books, during those periods."

441.   True popularity point of girls for men: Young > Pretty> Educated.

442.   A lot of girls don't know what they have temporarily – unwittingly waste their youth.

443.   The face is like a visual fingerprint.

444.   We don't have to show ours online, unless there is a clear benefit.

445.   "Why can't our teeth regenerate throughout our lives instead? They're the most high-maintenance part of our bodies." - A reddit user

446.   I think the human brain gets better even after 50. Walking has made me smarter.

447.   "A midlife crisis is when you're old enough to buy what you've always wanted but now have to decide if it was worth it." - A reddit user

448.   "You've already spent a final day with people you assumed you'd see again." This means we don't know when we will die – it can be much sooner than we think.

449.   "Most people can't name all of their great-grandparents. We'll basically be forgotten in 100 years." Which is why I am publishing a book now. Who knows if someone reads my books 500 years later and learns there was such a person existing once.

450.   "The 'richest people' list in actuality is the 'legally richest people', which is only close to the actual richest people list. There are tons of illegal super rich people." I have always thought about this – there are a lot of hidden riches in the world.

Author's Note

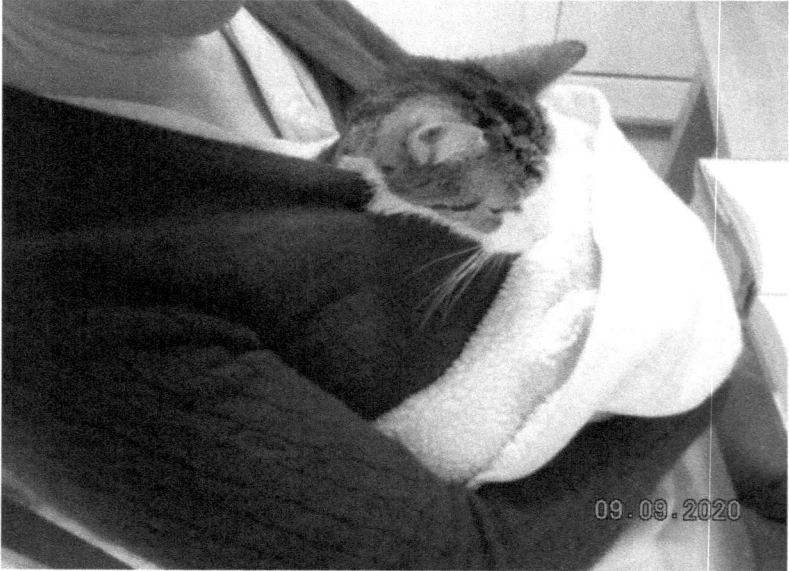

My wife is holding Oscar (2020).

I would appreciate a rating. *I do read all the reviews myself and try to learn from them.* I wish my best luck to you!

www.ingramcontent.com/pod-product-compliance
Lightning Source LLC
Chambersburg PA
CBHW032118280326
41933CB00009B/897